North Carolina Adventure Book

This book belongs to:

Call | Text this number if found:

My Nature Book Adventures

© 2023 My Nature Book Adventures - All Rights Reserved
www.mynaturebookadventures.com
1st Edition - 2023

© 2023 My Nature Book Adventures
All Rights Reserved
www.mynaturebookadventures.com

ISBN: 978-1-956162-78-3

Copyright © 2023

My Nature Book Adventures, LLC.

All Rights Reserved.
www.mynaturebookadventures.com

This publication, including all designs, photographs, and graphics used and/or depicted are protected under United States and international copyright laws and treaties, and may not be reproduced, publicly displayed, distributed, or derivative works prepared therefrom, without the prior express written permission of My Nature Book Adventures LLC. "My Nature Book Adventures" is a trademark owned by My Nature Book Adventures LLC.

Some images are used pursuant to license from Adobe Stock, Crella, and/or Canva and may not be further used, reproduced, publicly displayed, or distributed without the prior express written permission of the owners of such images.

If you wish to make any use of this publication other than for your own personal use, or to refer to brief excerpts for review purposes, please contact us through the above-referenced website.

https://www.mynaturebookadventures.com

Adventure Begins

The **North Carolina Adventure Book** is part planner, part journal, and 100% your adventure! Created to include dedicated space for you to plan your journey and share your experience. Check out each of the Parks and cross them off your MUST DO exploration list. Then look back at the experiences with your family and friends. Plan your adventures, then share all of the fun! Decorate your pages YOUR way.

Find your next adventure and share your treasured memories!

We have organized each destination on a map, making it easy to find the perfect location for you to explore. Each map has a pin to match the location of the destination to be used with the map key, showing exactly where you can find each location.

Spend your time surrounded in nature, taking in all of the unique beauty, and the beauty of exploring nature while visiting each one of these amazing destinations. Write about the special moments from each adventure inside.

You are creating your own special keepsake while making cherished lifelong memories.
.

Inside your book you will find...

ON THE LEFT SIDE OF EACH 2 PAGE SPREAD, YOU HAVE

- A place to plan the details of your trip.
- A would you return area
- An area to indicate how you felt during your trip
- A section for reservation information, including refund policy, reserved dates, address, check-in and check-out times, website, phone, wifi information, and even a place for your confirmation number.
- Plus an area to show how far you are traveling.
- An area for the places you discovered along the way
- Plus a dedicated section for places you want to stop at along the way
- A space to attach your favorite postcard, picture, drawing, stamp, decal and ticket stub.

THE RIGHT SIDE GIVES YOU A PLACE TO SHARE THE SPECIAL MOMENTS ABOUT EACH ONE OF YOUR JOURNEYS

Special Moments

- Include why you went
- Who went with you
- When you went
- What you did
- The souvenir you brought home
- What you saw
- What you learned
- A laughable moment
- A surprising moment
- An unforeseeable moment
- A list section
- A fun color-in of the weather you experienced during your adventures

Make it all about YOU and your journey!

Also inside is an adventure checklist to make your adventures even more memorable. And a QR code to online interactive maps for easy planning

We want you to spend your time enjoying each and every destination you get to visit in person.

SO WHAT ARE YOU WAITING FOR. IT'S TIME TO EXPLORE!

JAN

Day	Week
1	
2	
3	
4	01
5	
6	
7	
8	
9	
10	
11	02
12	
13	
14	
15	
16	
17	
18	03
19	
20	
21	
22	
23	
24	
25	04
26	
27	
28	
29	
30	
31	

FEB

Day	Week
1	05
2	
3	
4	
5	
6	
7	
8	06
9	
10	
11	
12	
13	
14	
15	07
16	
17	
18	
19	
20	
21	
22	08
23	
24	
25	
26	
27	
28	

MAR

Day	Week
1	09
2	
3	
4	
5	
6	
7	
8	10
9	
10	
11	
12	
13	
14	
15	11
16	
17	
18	
19	
20	
21	
22	12
23	
24	
25	
26	
27	
28	
29	13
30	
31	

APR	MAY	JUN
1	1	1
2	2	2 — 22
3	3 — 18	3
4	4	4
5 — 14	5	5
6	6	6
7	7	7 — 23
8	8	8
9	9	9
10	10 — 19	10
11	11	11
12 — 15	12	12
13	13	13
14	14	14 — 24
15	15	15
16	16	16
17	17 — 20	17
18	18	18
19 — 16	19	19
20	20	20
21	21	21 — 25
22	22	22
23	23	23
24	24 — 21	24
25	25	25
26 — 17	26	26
27	27	27
28	28	28 — 26
29	29	29
30	30	30
	31	

JUL	AUG	SEP
1	1	1
2	2 31	2
3	3	3
4	4	4
5 27	5	5
6	6	6 36
7	7	7
8	8	8
9	9 32	9
10	10	10
11	11	11
12 28	12	12
13	13	13 37
14	14	14
15	15	15
16	16 33	16
17	17	17
18	18	18
19 29	19	19
20	20	20 38
21	21	21
22	22	22
23	23 34	23
24	24	24
25	25	25
26 30	26	26
27	27	27 39
28	28	28
29	29	29
30	30 35	30
31	31	

OCT	NOV	DEC
1	1	1
2	2 44	2
3	3	3
4	4	4
5 40	5	5
6	6	6
7	7	7 49
8	8	8
9	9 45	9
10	10	10
11	11	11
12 41	12	12
13	13	13
14	14	14 50
15	15	15
16	16 46	16
17	17	17
18	18	18
19 42	19	19
20	20	20
21	21	21 51
22	22	22
23	23 47	23
24	24	24
25	25	25
26 43	26	26
27	27	27
28	28	28 52
29	29	29
30	30 48	30
31		31

Lake at Umstead State Park, North Carolina - Map #81

Chimney Rock State Park, North Carolina - Map #17

Deep Gap Trail, North Carolina

Adventure Checklist

- [ ] Go on a nature scavenger hunt
- [ ] Perfect your bird calls
- [ ] Have a breakfast picnic
- [ ] Go horseback riding
- [ ] Snap a selfie at a park entrance sign
- [ ] Help Someone become a Jr Ranger
- [ ] Go RVing
- [ ] Take a ranger-led tour
- [ ] Splash in a waterfall
- [ ] Stop at scenic overlooks
- [ ] Hunt for fossils
- [ ] Look for EarthCache sites
- [ ] Canoe along a river
- [ ] Go on a photography walk
- [ ] Take a nature hike
- [ ] Hunt for animal tracks
- [ ] Go kayaking
- [ ] Try rock climbing
- [ ] Visit a nature center
- [ ] Watch the sunset
- [ ] Ride a bike
- [ ] Try a night sky program
- [ ] Go geocaching
- [ ] Pitch a tent
- [ ] Photograph wildflowers

- [ ] Cast a fishing line
- [ ] Take a boat cruise across a lake
- [ ] Enjoy a scenic drive
- [ ] Snap lots of photos
- [ ] Smell the fresh air
- [ ] Arrive early for wildlife watching
- [ ] Scramble over rocks
- [ ] Eat a picnic at a scenic spot
- [ ] Go on a night hike
- [ ] Ride a historic train
- [ ] Hike to the top of a mountain
- [ ] Try a cell phone audio tour
- [ ] Enjoy a tidepool walk
- [ ] Go on a full moon ranger hike
- [ ] Go on a cave tour
- [ ] Go stargazing
- [ ] Adhere to Leave No Trace principles
- [ ] Play in the water

Mark the places on the map where you have visited. Be creative use a sticker, or just put a dot to mark your journey.

EXPLORE MORE

KENTUCKY

TENNESSEE

GEORGIA

SOUTH CAROLINA

my nature book adventures

North Carolina Map

Interactive Locations Map

View of Mile High Swinging Bridge, at Grandfather Mountain State Park, North Carolina.

Blue Ridge Parkway in the Fall

Great Smoky Mountains from Blue Ridge Parkway

Carolina Beach State Park -- Map #13
Type: State Parks | **Region:** Coast | **County:** New Hanover
Size: 761 acres (3.08 km2) | **Established:** 1969
1010 State Park Road, Carolina Beach, NC 28428
Phone: 910-458-8206 | **E-mail:** carolina.beach@ncparks.gov
Website: www.ncparks.gov/carolina-beach-state-park

Carvers Creek State Park -- Map #15
Type: State Parks | **Region:** Coastal Plain | **County:** Cumberland
Size: 4,530 acres (18.3 km2) | **Established:** 2005
Long Valley Farm access and park office, 2505 Long Valley Road, Spring Lake, NC 28390, GPS: 35.1970, -78.9767 | Sandhills access, 995 McCloskey Road, Fayetteville, NC 28311, GPS: 35.1700, -78.8943
Phone: 910-436-4681 | **E-mail:** carvers.creek@ncparks.gov
Website: www.ncparks.gov/carvers-creek-state-park

Chimney Rock State Park -- Map #17
Type: State Parks | **Region:** Mountains | **County:** Rutherford, Polk, Buncombe, Henderson
Size: 8,014 acres (32.43 km2) | **Established:** 2005
Chimney Rock access and park office, 743 Chimney Rock Park Road | Chimney Rock, NC 28720, GPS: 35.4327, -82.2502 | Rumbling Bald access, 827 Boys Camp Road, Lake Lure, NC 29746, GPS: 35.4434, -82.2194 Eagle Rock access, 1911 Shumont Road, Black Mountain, NC 28711, GPS: 35.4722, -82.2423
Phone: 828-625-1823 | **E-mail:** chimney.rock@ncparks.gov
Website: www.ncparks.gov/chimney-rock-state-park

Cliffs of the Neuse State Park -- Map #19
Type: State Parks | **Region:** Coastal Plain | **County:** Wayne
Size: 1,097 acres (4.44 km2) | **Established:** 1945
Visitor center, 240 Park Entrance Road, Seven Springs, NC 28578, GPS: 32.2354, -77.8932
Phone: 919-778-6234 | **E-mail:** cliffs.neuse@ncparks.gov
Website: www.ncparks.gov/cliffs-of-the-neuse-state-park

Crowders Mountain State Park -- Map #21
Type: State Parks | **Region:** Piedmont | **County:** Gaston
Size: 5,217 acres (21.11 km2) | **Established:** 1973

Sparrow Springs access and visitor center, 522 Park Office Lane, Kings Mountain, NC 28086, GPS: 35.2133, -81.2935 | Linwood Road access, 4611 Linwood Road, Gastonia, NC 28086, GPS: 35.2409, -81.2693 | Boulders access, 108 Van Dyke Road, Kings Mountain, NC 28086, GPS: 35.1711, -81.3627
Phone: 704-853-5375 | **E-mail:** crowders.mountain@ncparks.gov
Website: www.ncparks.gov/crowders-mountain-state-park

Dismal Swamp State Park -- Map #23
Type: State Parks | **Region:** Coastal Plain | **County:** Camden
Size: 14,432 acres (58.40 km2) | **Established:** 1974

Visitor center, 2294 U.S. 17 N., South Mills, NC 27976, GPS: 36.5057, -76.3551
Phone: 252-771-6593 | **E-mail:** dismal.swamp@ncparks.gov
Website: www.ncparks.gov/dismal-swamp-state-park

Elk Knob State Park -- Map #25
Type: State Parks | **Region:** Mountains | **County:** Watauga, Ashe
Size: 4,423 acres (17.90 km2) | **Established:** 2002

Park office, 5564 Meat Camp Road, Todd, NC 28684, GPS: 36.3325, -81.6906
Phone: 828-297-7261 | **E-mail:** elk.knob@ncparks.gov
Website: www.ncparks.gov/elk-knob-state-park

Eno River State Park -- Map #27
Type: State Parks | **Region:** Piedmont | **County:** Durham, Orange
Size: 4,319 acres (17.48 km2) | **Established:** 1973

Fews Ford access and park office, 6101 Cole Mill Road, Durham, NC 27705, GPS: 36.0783, -79.0050 | Cabelands access, 4950 Howe St., Durham, NC 27705, GPS: 36.0400, -78.9888 | Cole Mill access, 4390 Old Cole Mill Road, Durham, NC 27712, GPS: 36.0599, -78.9804 | Pleasant Green access, 4770 Pleasant Green Road, Durham, NC 27705, GPS: 36.0459, -79.0115 | Pump Station access, 4023 Rivermont Road, Durham, NC 27712, GPS: 36.0594, -78.9652
Phone: 919-383-1686 | **E-mail:** eno.river@ncparks.gov
Website: www.ncparks.gov/eno-river-state-park

Fort Macon State Park -- Map #29
Type: State Parks | **Region:** Coast | **County:** Carteret
Size: 424 acres (1.72 km2) | **Established:** 1924
Visitor center, 2303 E. Fort Macon Road, Atlantic Beach, NC 28512, GPS: 34.6979, -76.6783
Phone: 252-726-3775 | **E-mail:** fort.macon@ncparks.gov
Website: www.ncparks.gov/fort-macon-state-park

Goose Creek State Park -- Map #31
Type: State Parks | **Region:** Coastal Plain | **County:** Beaufort
Size: 1,672 acres (6.77 km2) | **Established:** 1974
Visitor center, 2190 Camp Leach Road, Washington, NC 27889, GPS: 35.4818, -76.9014
Phone: 252-923-2191 | **E-mail:** goose.creek@ncparks.gov
Website: www.ncparks.gov/goose-creek-state-park

Gorges State Park -- Map #33
Type: State Parks | **Region:** Mountains | **County:** Transylvania
Size: 7,709 acres (31.20 km2) | **Established:** 1999
Visitor center, 976 Grassy Ridge Road, Sapphire, NC 28774, GPS: 35.0960, -82.9510 | Frozen Creek access, Frozen Creek Road, Brevard, NC 28712, GPS: 35.1086, -82.8837
Phone: 828-966-9099 | **E-mail:** gorges@ncparks.gov
Website: www.ncparks.gov/gorges-state-park

Grandfather Mountain State Park -- Map #35
Type: State Parks | **Region:** Mountains | **County:** Avery, Watauga, Caldwell
Size: 3,647 acres (14.76 km2) | **Established:** 2009
Park office, 9872 N.C. 105 S., Suite 6, Banner Elk, NC 28604, GPS: 36.1549, -81.7872 | Profile Trail parking area, 4198 N.C. 105 N., Banner Elk, NC 28604, GPS: 36.1197, -81.8350
Phone: 828-963-9522 | **E-mail:** grandfather.mountain@ncparks.gov
Website: www.ncparks.gov/grandfather-mountain-state-park

Hammocks Beach State Park -- Map #37
Type: State Parks | **Region:** Coast | **County:** Onslow
Size: 1,611 acres (6.52 km2) | **Established:** 1961

Visitor center, 1572 Hammock Beach Road, Swansboro, NC 28584, GPS: 34.6710, -77.1429
Phone: 910-326-4881 | **E-mail:** hammocks.beach@ncparks.gov
Website: www.ncparks.gov/hammocks-beach-state-park

Hanging Rock State Park -- Map #39
Type: State Parks | **Region:** Piedmont | **County:** Stokes
Size: 9,011 acres (36.47 km2) | **Established:** 1935

Park entrance, 1790 Hanging Rock Park Road, Danbury, NC 27016, GPS: 36.4119, -80.2541 | Visitor center, 1005 Visitor Center Drive, Westfield, NC 27053, GPS: 36.3952, -80.2665 | Lake bathhouse, 2847 Hanging Rock Park Road, Westfield, NC 27053, GPS: 36.3902, -80.2678 | Lower Cascades parking area, 2143 Hall Road, Westfield, NC 27053, GPS: 36.4148, -80.2647 | Dan River access, 1258 Flinchum Road, Danbury, NC 27016, GPS: 36.4293, -80.2487 | Tory's Den parking area, 1185 Charlie Young Road, Westfield, NC 27053, GPS: 36.4019, -80.2995 | Climbing access, 1035 Climbing Access Drive, Westfield, NC 27053, GPS: 36.3995, -80.2906 | Mountain biking access, 2568 Moores Spring Road, Westfield, NC 27053, GPS: 36.4187, -80.2839
Phone: 336-593-8480 | **E-mail:** hanging.rock@ncparks.gov
Website: www.ncparks.gov/hanging-rock-state-park

Haw River State Park -- Map #41
Type: State Parks | **Region:** Piedmont | **County:** Rockingham, Guilford
Size: 1,485 acres (6.01 km2) | **Established:** 2003

The Summit Center and park office, 339 Conference Center Drive, Browns Summit, NC 27214, GPS: 36.2508, -79.7563 | Iron Ore Belt access, 6068 N. Church St., Greensboro, NC 27455, GPS: 36.2374, -79.7855
Phone: 336-342-6163 | **E-mail:** haw.river@ncparks.gov
Website: www.ncparks.gov/haw-river-state-park

Jockey's Ridge State Park -- Map #43
Type: State Parks | **Region:** Coast | **County:** Dare
Size: 427 acres (1.73 km2) | **Established:** 1975

Visitor center, 300 W. Carolista Drive, Nags Head, NC 27959, GPS: 35.9642, -75.6330 | Soundside access, 330 W. Soundside Road, Nags Head, NC 27959, GPS: 35.9525, -75.6320
Phone: 252-441-7132 | **E-mail:** jockeys.ridge@ncparks.gov
Website: www.ncparks.gov/jockeys-ridge-state-park

Jones Lake State Park -- Map #45
Type: State Parks | **Region:** Coastal Plain | **County:** Bladen
Size: 1,669 acres (6.75 km2) | **Established:** 1939
Visitor center, 4117 N.C. 242 N., Elizabethtown, NC 28337, GPS: 34.6827, -78.5954
Phone: 910-588-4550 | **E-mail:** jones.lake@ncparks.gov
Website: www.ncparks.gov/jones-lake-state-park

Lake James State Park -- Map #47
Type: State Parks | **Region:** Mountains | **County:** McDowell, Burke
Size: 3,743 acres (15.15 km2) | **Established:** 1987
Paddy's Creek access, 7321 N.C. 126, Nebo, NC 28761, GPS: 35.7503, -81.8920 | Catawba River access and park office, 2785 N.C. 126, Nebo, NC 28761, GPS: 35.7287, -81.9011 | Hidden Cove boat ramp, 3381 N.C. 126, Nebo, NC 28761, GPS: 35.7301, -81.8908 | Canal Bridge boat ramp, 9182 N.C. 126, Nebo, NC 28761, GPS: 35.7394, -81.8863
Phone: 828-584-7728 | **E-mail:** lake.james@ncparks.gov
Website: www.ncparks.gov/lake-james-state-park

Lake Norman State Park -- Map #49
Type: State Parks | **Region:** Piedmont | **County:** Iredell
Size: 1,942 acres (7.86 km2) | **Established:** 1962
Visitor center, 759 State Park Road, Troutman, NC 28166, GPS: 35.6725, -80.9325
Phone: 704-528-6350 | **E-mail:** lake.norman@ncparks.gov
Website: www.ncparks.gov/lake-norman-state-park

Lake Waccamaw State Park -- Map #51
Type: State Parks | **Region:** Coastal Plain | **County:** Columbus
Size: 2,398 acres (9.70 km2) | **Established:** 1976
Visitor center, 1866 State Park Drive, Lake Waccamaw, NC 28450, GPS: 34.2790, -78.4654
Phone: 910-646-4748 | **E-mail:** lake.waccamaw@ncparks.gov
Website: www.ncparks.gov/lake-waccamaw-state-park

Lumber River State Park -- Map #53
Type: State Parks | **Region:** Coastal Plain | **County:** Scotland, Hoke, Robeson, Columbus
Size: 13,695 acres (55.42 km2) | **Established:** 1989

Princess Ann access and park office, 2819 Princess Ann Road, Orrum, NC 28369, GPS: 34.390023, -79.00222 | Chalk Banks access, 26040 Raeford Road, Wagram, NC 28396, GPS: 34.898889, -79.354889
Phone: 910-628-4564 | **E-mail:** lumber.river@ncparks.gov
Website: www.ncparks.gov/lumber-river-state-park

Mayo River State Park -- Map #55
Type: State Parks | **Region:** Piedmont | **County:** Rockingham
Size: 2,778 acres (11.24 km2) | **Established:** 2003

Mayo Mountain access and park office, 500 Old Mayo Park Road, Mayodan, NC 27027, GPS: 36.4391, -79.9475 | Deshazo Mill access, 113 Deshazo Road (off of Anglin Mill Road), Stoneville, NC 27048, GPS: 36.5362, -79.9940 | Anglin Mill access, Old Anglin Road/Mayo Beach Road (off of Anglin Mill Road), Stoneville, NC 27048, GPS: 36.5296, -79.9894 | Hickory Creek access, Tyne Road (off of Bennet Road), Stoneville, NC 27048, GPS: 36.5093, -79.9984 | Mayodan access, N.C. 135 (at Cedar Mountain Road), Mayodan, NC 27027, GPS: 36.4073, -79.9650
Phone: 336-427-2530 | **E-mail:** mayo.river@ncparks.gov
Website: www.ncparks.gov/mayo-river-state-park

Medoc Mountain State Park -- Map #57
Type: State Parks | **Region:** Piedmont | **County:** Halifax
Size: 3,893 acres (15.75 km2) | **Established:** 1973

Visitor center, 1541 Medoc State Park Road, Hollister, NC 27844, GPS: 36.2639, -77.8883
Phone: 252-586-6588 | **E-mail:** medoc.mountain@ncparks.gov
Website: www.ncparks.gov/medoc-mountain-state-park

Merchants Millpond State Park -- Map #59
Type: State Parks | **Region:** Coastal Plain | **County:** Gates
Size: 3,520 acres (14.2 km2) | **Established:** 1973

Visitor center, 176 Millpond Road, Gatesville, NC 27938, GPS: 36.4371, -76.7016
Phone: 252-357-1191 | **E-mail:** merchants.millpond@ncparks.gov
Website: www.ncparks.gov/merchants-millpond-state-park

Morrow Mountain State Park -- Map #61
Type: State Parks | **Region:** Piedmont | **County:** Stanly
Size: 5,702 acres (23.08 km2) | **Established:** 1935

Park office, 49104 Morrow Mountain Road, Albemarle, NC 28001, GPS: 35.3737, -80.0735
Phone: 704-982-4402 | **E-mail:** morrow.mountain@ncparks.gov
Website: www.ncparks.gov/morrow-mountain-state-park

Mount Mitchell State Park -- Map #63
Type: State Parks | **Region:** Mountains | **County:** Yancey
Size: 4,789 acres (19.38 km2) | **Established:** 1916

Park office, 2388 N.C. 128, Burnsville, NC 28714, GPS: 35.7528, -82.2737
Phone: 828-675-4611 | **E-mail:** mount.mitchell@ncparks.gov
Website: www.ncparks.gov/mount-mitchell-state-park

New River State Park -- Map #65
Type: State Parks | **Region:** Mountains | **County:** Alleghany, Ashe
Size: 3,323 acres (13.45 km2) | **Established:** 1975

U.S. 221 access and visitor center, 358 New River State Park Road, Laurel Springs, NC 28644, GPS: 36.4676, -81.3403 | Wagoner access, 1477 Wagoner Access Road, Jefferson, NC 28640, GPS: 36.4158, -81.3871 | Kings Creek access, 2250 Kings Creek Road, Piney Creek, NC 28663, GPS: 36.5276, -81.3363 | Elk Shoals access, 349 Methodist Camp Road, West Jefferson, NC 28694, GPS: 36.3653, -81.4332
Phone: 336-982-2587 | **E-mail:** new.river@ncparks.gov
Website: www.ncparks.gov/new-river-state-park

Pettigrew State Park -- Map #67
Type: State Parks | **Region:** Coastal Plain | **County:** Tyrrell, Washington
Size: 5,951 acres (24.08 km2) | **Established:** 1936

Park office, 2252 Lake Shore Road, Creswell, NC 27928, GPS: 35.7889, -76.4038
Phone: 252-797-4475 | **E-mail:** pettigrew@ncparks.gov
Website: www.ncparks.gov/pettigrew-state-park

Pilot Mountain State Park -- Map #69
Type: State Parks | **Region:** Piedmont | **County:** Surry, Yadkin
Size: 3,872 acres (15.67 km2) | **Established:** 1968

Mountain section and visitor center, 1792 Pilot Knob Park Road, Pinnacle, NC 27043, GPS: 36.3412, -80.4629 | Pilot Creek access, 382 Boyd Nelson Road, Pinnacle, NC 27043, GPS: 36.3587, -80.4933 | Pinnacle Hotel Road/Culler Road parking, 134 Culler Road, Pinnacle, NC 27043, GPS: 36.3280, -80.4631 | Hauser Road parking, 622 Hauser Road, Pinnacle, NC 27043, GPS: 36.2675, -80.4958 | Bean Shoals access, 103 Yadkin River Park Trail, Pinnacle, NC 27043, GPS: 36.2647, -80.4878 | Ivy Bluff access, 4240 Shoals Road, East Bend, NC 27018, GPS: 36.2537, -80.5087 | Shoals fishing area and paddle access, 4454 Shoals Road, East Bend, NC 27018 GPS: 36.2574, -80.5171
Phone: 336-444-5100 | **E-mail:** pilot.mountain@ncparks.gov
Website: www.ncparks.gov/pilot-mountain-state-park

Pisgah View State Park -- Map #71
Type: State Parks | **Region:** Mountains | **County:** Buncombe, Haywood[12]
Size: 205 acres (0.83 km2) | **Established:** 2019

Phone: | **E-mail:**
Website:

Raven Rock State Park -- Map #73
Type: State Parks | **Region:** Piedmont | **County:** Harnett
Size: 4,810 acres (19.5 km2) | **Established:** 1970

Visitor center, 3009 Raven Rock Road, Lillington, NC 27546, GPS: 35.4597, -78.9127 | Moccasin Branch access, 814 Moccasin Branch Road, Lillington, NC 27546, GPS: 35.4549, -78.9081
Phone: 910-893-4888 | **E-mail:** raven.rock@ncparks.gov
Website: www.ncparks.gov/raven-rock-state-park

Singletary Lake State Park -- Map #75
Type: State Parks | **Region:** Coastal Plain | **County:** Bladen
Size: 649 acres (2.63 km2) | **Established:** 1939

Park office, 6707 N.C. 53 E., Kelly, NC 28448, GPS: 34.5831, -78.4496
Phone: 910-669-2928 | **E-mail:** singletary.lake@ncparks.gov
Website: www.ncparks.gov/singletary-lake-state-park

South Mountains State Park -- Map #77
Type: State Parks | **Region:** Mountains | **County:** Burke
Size: 20,949 acres (84.78 km2) | **Established:** 1978

Jacob Fork access and visitor center, 3001 South Mountain Park Ave., Connelly Springs, NC 28612, GPS: 35.5963, -81.6000 | Clear Creek access, (day-use only), 5999 Branstrom Orchard St., Morganton, NC 28655, GPS: 35.6424, -81.7524

Phone: 828-433-4772 | **E-mail:** south.mountains@ncparks.gov
Website: www.ncparks.gov/south-mountains-state-park

Stone Mountain State Park -- Map #79
Type: State Parks | **Region:** Mountains | **County:** Alleghany, Wilkes
Size: 14,353 acres (58.08 km2) | **Established:** 1969

Park office, 3042 Frank Parkway, Roaring Gap, NC 28668, GPS: 36.3873, -81.0273

Phone: 336-957-8185 | **E-mail:** stone.mountain@ncparks.gov
Website: www.ncparks.gov/stone-mountain-state-park

William B. Umstead State Park -- Map #81
Type: State Parks | **Region:** Piedmont | **County:** Wake
Size: 5,599 acres (22.66 km2) | **Established:** 1945

Crabtree Creek access and visitor center, 8801 Glenwood Ave., Raleigh, NC 27617, GPS: 35.8905, -78.7502 | Reedy Creek access, 2100 N. Harrison Ave., Cary, NC 27513, GPS: 35.8334, -78.7603

Phone: 984-867-8240 | **E-mail:** william.umstead@ncparks.gov
Website: www.ncparks.gov/william-b-umstead-state-park

Falls Lake State Recreation Area -- Map #85
Type: State Recreation Areas | **Region:** Piedmont | **County:** Wake, Durham
Size: 5,035 acres (20.38 km2) | **Established:** 1982

Visitor center, 13304 Creedmoor Road, Wake Forest, NC 27587, GPS: 36.0116, -78.6888 | Beaverdam, 14600 Creedmoor Road, Wake Forest, NC 27587, GPS: 36.0362, -78.6850 | B.W. Wells campground, 1630 Bent Road, Wake Forest, NC 27587, GPS: 35.9861, -78.6315 | Highway 50, 13900 Creedmoor Road, Wake Forest, NC 27587, GPS: 36.0216, -78.6902 | Holly Point campground, 14424 New Light Road, Wake Forest, NC 27587, GPS: 36.0100, -78.6575 | Rolling View, 4201 Baptist Road, Durham, NC 27703, GPS: 36.0085, -78.7291 | Sandling Beach, 14601 Creedmoor Road, Wake Forest, NC 27587, GPS: 36.0423, -78.6984 | Shinleaf campground, 13708 New Light Road, Wake Forest, NC 27587, GPS: 35.9938, -78.6595

Phone: 984-867-8000 | **E-mail:** falls.lake@ncparks.gov
Website: www.ncparks.gov/falls-lake-state-recreation-area

Fort Fisher State Recreation Area -- Map #87
Type: State Recreation Areas | **Region:** Coast | **County:** New Hanover
Size: 287 acres (1.16 km2) | **Established:** 1986

Park office, 1000 Loggerhead Road, Kure Beach, NC 28449, GPS: 33.9534, -77.9290

Phone: 910-458-5798 | **E-mail:** fort.fisher@ncparks.gov
Website: www.ncparks.gov/fort-fisher-state-recreation-area

Jordan Lake State Recreation Area -- Map #89
Type: State Recreation Areas | **Region:** Piedmont | **County:** Chatham
Size: 4,558 acres (18.45 km2) | **Established:** 1981

Visitor center, 280 State Park Road, Apex, NC 27523, GPS: 35.7355, -79.0165 | Crosswinds campground, 389 Farrington Road, Apex, NC 27502, GPS: 35.7420, -79.0021 | Ebenezer Church, 2582 Beaver Creek Road, Apex, NC 27502, GPS: 35.7082, -79.0157 | New Hope Overlook, 339 W.H. Jones Road, New Hill, NC 27562, GPS: 35.6772, -79.0454 | Parkers Creek campground, Parkers Creek Beach Road, Chapel Hill, NC 27517, GPS: 35.7381, -79.0410 | Poplar Point campground, 558 Beaver Creek Road, Apex, NC 27502, GPS: 35.7289, -79.0044 | Seaforth, Seaforth Beach Road, Pittsboro, NC 27312, GPS: 35.7354, -79.0380 | Vista Point campground, 2498 N. Pea Ridge Road, Pittsboro, NC 27312, GPS: 35.7094, -79.0592 | White Oak recreation area, White Oak Beach Road, Apex, NC 27523, GPS: 35.7384, -79.0122

Phone: 919-362-0586 | **E-mail:** jordan.lake@ncparks.gov
Website: www.ncparks.gov/jordan-lake-state-recreation-area

Kerr Lake State Recreation Area -- Map #91
Type: State Recreation Areas | **Region:** Piedmont | **County:** Vance, Warren
Size: 3,376 acres (13.66 km2) | **Established:** 1952

Satterwhte Point and Visitors Center, 6254 Satterwhite Point Road, Henderson, NC 27537, GPS: 36.4411, -78.3688 J.C. Cooper Campground, 20 Shoreline Lane, Henderson, NC 27537, GPS: 36.4411, -78.3688 Bullocksville, 3050 Bullocksville Park Rd, Manson, NC 27553, GPS: 36.4577, -78.3631 County Line, 200 County Line Park Road, Manson, NC 27553, GPS: 36.5247, -78.3163 Henderson Point, 1427 Reverend Henderson Rd, Henderson, NC 27537, GPS: 36.5312, -78.3461 Hibernia, 2041 Hibernia Road, Henderson, NC 27537, GPS: 36.5047, -78.3761 Kimball Point, 460 Kimball Point Road, Manson, NC 27553, GPS: 36.5367, -78.3099 Nutbush Bridge, North entrance, 115 Jack Wade Farm Lane, Henderson, NC 27537, South entrance, 135 Jack Wade Farm Lane, Henderson, NC 27537, GPS: 36.4100, -78.3991

Phone: 252-438-7791 | **E-mail:** kerr.lake@ncparks.gov
Website: www.ncparks.gov/kerr-lake-state-recreation-area

Backbone Ridge State Forest -- Map #95
Type: NORTH CAROLINA STATE FORESTS | **Region:** Mountains | **County:** Caldwell
Size: 476 acres (1.93 km2) | **Note:** No public access

Milepost: 300

Phone: 919.828.4199 | **E-mail:** www.ctnc.org/
Website: https://protecttheblueridgeparkway.org/property/backbone-ridge/

Bladen Lakes State Forest -- Map #97
Type: NORTH CAROLINA STATE FORESTS | **Region:** Coastal Plain | **County:** Bladen

Size: 32,700 acres (132 km2) | **Hours/Operation:** Open year-round via permit

4470 NC Highway 242 N, Elizabethtown, NC 28337-6740
Phone: 910-588-4964 | **E-mail:** hans.rohr@ncagr.gov
Website: ncforestservice.gov/Contacts/blsf.htm

Clemmons Educational State Forest -- Map #99
Type: NORTH CAROLINA STATE FORESTS | **Region:** Piedmont | **County:** Johnston, Wake

Size: 825 acres (3.34 km2) |
Hours/Operation: Open March through November

2411 Old U.S. 70 West, Clayton, N.C. 27520
Phone: 919-553-5651 | **E-mail:** ClemmonsESF.ncfs@ncagr.gov
Website: https://www.ncesf.org/clemmons.html

DuPont State Recreational Forest -- Map #101
Type: NORTH CAROLINA STATE FORESTS | **Region:** Mountains | **County:** Henderson, Transylvania

Size: 10,473 acres (42.38 km2) | **Hours/Operation:** Open year-round

89 Buck Forest Rd, Cedar Mountain, NC 28718
Phone: 828-877-6527 | **E-mail:** dupontsf.ncfs@ncagr.gov
Website: https://www.dupontstaterecreationalforest.com/

Gill State Forest -- Map #103
Type: NORTH CAROLINA STATE FORESTS | **Region:** Mountains | **County:** Avery

Size: 474 acres (1.92 km2) |
Hours/Operation: Not open to the general public

Headwaters State Forest -- Map #105
Type: NORTH CAROLINA STATE FORESTS | **Region:** Mountains | **County:** Transylvania
Size: 6,730 acres (27.2 km2) | **Hours/Operation:** Open year-round

14 Gaston Mountain Road, Asheville, NC 28806
Phone: 828-665-8688 | **E-mail:** headwaterssf.ncfs@ncagr.gov
Website: https://www.ncforestservice.gov/Headwaters/index.htm

---

Holmes Educational State Forest -- Map #107
Type: NORTH CAROLINA STATE FORESTS | **Region:** Mountains | **County:** Henderson
Size: 235 acres (0.95 km2) |
Hours/Operation: Open March through November

1299 Crab Creek Road, Hendersonville, N.C., 28739
Phone: (828) 692-0100 | **E-mail:** holmesESF.ncfs@ncagr.gov
Website: https://www.ncesf.org/holmes.html

Jordan Lake Educational State Forest -- Map #109
Type: NORTH CAROLINA STATE FORESTS | **Region:** Piedmont | **County:** Chatham
Size: 900 acres (3.6 km2) |
Hours/Operation: Open March through November

2832 Big Woods Road, Chapel Hill, NC 27517
Phone: (919) 542-1154 | **E-mail:** JordanLakeESF.ncfs@ncagr.gov
Website: https://www.ncesf.org/jordanlake.html

Mountain Island Educational State Forest -- Map #111
Type: NORTH CAROLINA STATE FORESTS | **Region:** Piedmont | **County:** Lincoln, Gaston
Size: 2,000 acres (8.1 km2) |
Hours/Operation: Only open for scheduled guided tours

534 Killian Road, Stanley, NC 28164
Phone: (704) 822-9518 | **E-mail:** mountainislandESF.ncfs@ncagr.gov
Website: https://www.ncesf.org/mtIsland.html

Rendezvous Mountain Educational State Forest -- Map #113
Type: NORTH CAROLINA STATE FORESTS | **Region:** Mountains | **County:** Wilkes **Size:** 3,316 acres (13.42 km2) |
Hours/Operation: Open March through November

Rendezvous Mountain Educational State Forest was allocated as part of the Rendezvous Mountain Park grant to the Department of Natural and Cultural Resources. This action was directed by the Legislature as part of the state budget approved during the 2021-2022 session. The transferred land will become part of the State Parks system as a satellite annex of Stone Mountain State Park and is no longer operating under the management of the N.C. Forest Service. | For information about Stone Mountain State Park and/or Rendezvous Mountain State Park, visit www.ncparks.gov.

Website: https://www.ncesf.org/rendezvousMt.html

Turnbull Creek Educational State Forest -- Map #115
Type: NORTH CAROLINA STATE FORESTS | **Region:** Coastal Plain | **County:** Bladen
Size: 890 acres (3.6 km2) | **Hours/Operation:** Open March through November
4803 Sweet Home Church Rd., Elizabethtown, NC 28337
Phone: (910) 588-4161 | **E-mail:** turnbullcreekESF.ncfs@ncagr.gov
Website: https://www.ncesf.org/turnbull.html

Tuttle Educational State Forest -- Map #117
Type: NORTH CAROLINA STATE FORESTS | **Region:** Mountains | **County:** Caldwell
Size: 288 acres (1.17 km2) |
Hours/Operation: Open March through November
3420 Playmore Beach Road, Lenoir, NC 28645
Phone: (828) 757-5608 | **E-mail:** tuttleESF.ncfs@ncagr.gov
Website: https://www.ncesf.org/tuttle/home.html

Dan River State Trail -- Map #147
Type: State Trails
Established: 2021
still in development
Phone: 919-707-9300 | **E-mail:** trails@ncparks.gov
Website: https://trails.nc.gov/state-trails/dan-river-state-trail

Deep River State Trail -- Map #149
Type: State Trails | **Region:** Piedmont
Size: 1,274 acres (5.16 km2)

Phone: 919-707-9300 | **E-mail:** trails@ncparks.gov
Website: https://trails.nc.gov/state-trails/deep-river-state-trail

East Coast Greenway State Trail -- Map #151
Type: State Trails

Phone: 919-707-9300 | **E-mail:** trails@ncparks.gov
Website: https://trails.nc.gov/state-trails/east-coast-greenway-state-trail

Fonta Flora State Trail -- Map #153
Type: State Trails | **Region:** Mountains
Size: 19 miles (31 km)

Phone: 919-707-9300 | **E-mail:** trails@ncparks.gov
Website: https://trails.nc.gov/state-trails/fonta-flora-state-trail

French Broad River State Trail -- Map #155
Type: State Trails | **Region:** Mountains
Size: 117 miles (188 km)

Phone: 919-707-9300 | **E-mail:** trails@ncparks.gov
Website: https://trails.nc.gov/state-trails/french-broad-river-state-trail

Hickory Nut Gorge State Trail -- Map #157
Type: State Trails | **Region:** Mountains

Phone: 919-707-9300 | **E-mail:** trails@ncparks.gov
Website: https://trails.nc.gov/state-trails/hickory-nut-gorge-state-trail

---

Mountains-to-Sea State Park Trail -- Map #159
Type: State Trails
Size: 669 miles (1,077 km)

Phone: 919-707-9300 | **E-mail:** trails@ncparks.gov
Website: https://trails.nc.gov/state-trails/mountains-sea-state-trail

---

Northern Peaks State Trail -- Map #161
Type: State Trails | **Region:** Mountains

Phone: 919-707-9300 | **E-mail:** trails@ncparks.gov
Website: https://trails.nc.gov/state-trails/northern-peaks-state-trail

---

Overmountain Victory State Trail -- Map #163
Type: State Trails | **Region:** Mountains
Size: 49.5 miles (79.7 km)

Phone: 919-707-9300 | **E-mail:** trails@ncparks.gov
Website: https://trails.nc.gov/state-trails/overmountain-victory-state-trail

View of Mile High Swinging Bridge, at Grandfather Mountain State Park, North Carolina.

Stone Mountain State Park - Map #79

Pisgah View State Park -- Map #71

Roanoke River State Trail -- Map #165
Type: State Trails

Phone: 919-707-9300 | **E-mail:** trails@ncparks.gov
Website: https://trails.nc.gov/state-trails/roanoke-river-state-trail

Wilderness Gateway State Trail -- Map #167
Type: State Trails | **Region:** Mountains

Phone: 919-707-9300 | **E-mail:** trails@ncparks.gov
Website: https://trails.nc.gov/state-trails/wilderness-gateway-state-trail

Yadkin River State Trail -- Map #169
Type: State Trails | **Region:** Piedmont
Size: 130 miles (210 km)

Phone: 919-707-9300 | **E-mail:** trails@ncparks.gov
Website: https://trails.nc.gov/state-trails/yadkin-river-state-trail

Fort Macon State Park -- Map #29

Plan Your Trip:

☐ Trip Plan Completed
☐ Day Trip   ☐ Overnight Stay
Reservations required: ☐ y ☐ n
Date reservations made: _____
Confirmation #: _____
Dog friendly?: ☐ y ☐ n

Destination Information:

_____
_____

Places we discovered along the way
_____
_____
_____

Places to stop and see along the way
_____
_____

Goals:

☐ _____
☐ _____
☐ _____
☐ _____
☐ _____
☐ _____

Would you go again?: ☐ y ☐ n   Open all year?: ☐ y ☐ n

How I felt: ☺ ☺ ☺ ☹ ☹

☐ _____
☐ _____
☐ _____
☐ _____
☐ _____

Add your favorite ticket stub, postcard, photo, stamp, decals or drawings here

www.mynaturebookadventures.com

DESTINATION:

S M T W T F S

Season Visited

Star Rating
☆☆☆☆☆

My favorite souvenir...
My favorite thing about this place is...

Why I went ...
Who I went with ...
When I went ...

What I did...
What I saw...

What I learned...

A laughable moment...

A surprising moment...

An unforeseeable moment...

My List
- ☐
- ☐
- ☐
- ☐
- ☐
- ☐
- ☐
- ☐
- ☐
- ☐
- ☐
- ☐

Snapped a selfie | Location...
Took a park sign selfie? - Y | N   The weather was ...

www.mynaturebookadventures.com

Plan Your Trip:

☐ Trip Plan Completed
☐ Day Trip ☐ Overnight Stay
Reservations required: ☐ y ☐ n
Date reservations made: _____
Confirmation #: _____
Dog friendly?: ☐ y ☐ n

Places to stop and see along the way

Goals:

☐ _____
☐ _____
☐ _____
☐ _____
☐ _____
☐ _____

Destination Information:

Places we discovered along the way

Would you go again?: ☐ y ☐ n   Open all year?: ☐ y ☐ n

How I felt: 😊😊😐☹️😖

☐ _____
☐ _____
☐ _____
☐ _____
☐ _____

Add your favorite ticket stub, postcard, photo, stamp, decals or drawings here

www.mynaturebookadventures.com

DESTINATION:

S M T W T F S

Season Visited

Star Rating

My favorite souvenir...
My favorite thing about this place is...

Why I went ...
Who I went with ...
When I went ...

What I did...
What I saw...

My List

What I learned...

A laughable moment...

A surprising moment...

An unforeseeable moment...

Snapped a selfie | Location...
Took a park sign selfie? - Y | N   The weather was ...

www.mynaturebookadventures.com

Plan Your Trip:

- ☐ Trip Plan Completed
- ☐ Day Trip   ☐ Overnight Stay

Reservations required: ☐ y ☐ n
Date reservations made: _____
Confirmation #: _____
Dog friendly?: ☐ y ☐ n

Destination Information:

_____
_____

Places we discovered along the way

_____
_____
_____

Places to stop and see along the way

_____
_____

Goals:

- ☐ _____
- ☐ _____
- ☐ _____
- ☐ _____
- ☐ _____
- ☐ _____

Would you go again?: ☐ y ☐ n   Open all year?: ☐ y ☐ n

How I felt: 😊 🙂 😐 🙁 ☹️

- ☐ _____
- ☐ _____
- ☐ _____
- ☐ _____
- ☐ _____

Add your favorite ticket stub, postcard, photo, stamp, decals or drawings here

www.mynaturebookadventures.com

DESTINATION:

S M T W T F S

Season Visited

_____
Star Rating
☆☆☆☆☆

My favorite souvenir... _____
My favorite thing about this place is... _____

_____
Why I went ... _____
Who I went with ... _____
When I went ... _____

_____
What I did... _____
What I saw... _____

_____
What I learned... _____
_____
_____

A laughable moment... _____
_____
_____
_____

A surprising moment... _____
_____
_____
_____

An unforeseeable moment... _____
_____
_____

My List
- ☐ _____
- ☐ _____
- ☐ _____
- ☐ _____
- ☐ _____
- ☐ _____
- ☐ _____
- ☐ _____
- ☐ _____
- ☐ _____
- ☐ _____

Snapped a selfie | Location... _____
Took a park sign selfie? - Y | N   The weather was ...

www.mynaturebookadventures.com

Plan Your Trip:

- ☐ Trip Plan Completed
- ☐ Day Trip   ☐ Overnight Stay

Reservations required: ☐ y ☐ n
Date reservations made: _____
Confirmation #: _____
Dog friendly?: ☐ y ☐ n

Destination Information:

_____

Places we discovered along the way

_____
_____
_____
_____

Places to stop and see along the way

_____
_____

Goals:

- ☐ _____
- ☐ _____
- ☐ _____
- ☐ _____
- ☐ _____
- ☐ _____

Would you go again?: ☐ y ☐ n   Open all year?: ☐ y ☐ n

How I felt: ☺ ☺ ☹ ☹

- ☐ _____
- ☐ _____
- ☐ _____
- ☐ _____
- ☐ _____

Add your favorite ticket stub, postcard, photo, stamp, decals or drawings here

www.mynaturebookadventures.com

DESTINATION:

S M T W T F S

Season Visited

_____
Star Rating
☆☆☆☆☆

My favorite souvenir...
My favorite thing about this place is...

Why I went ...
Who I went with ...
When I went ...

What I did...
What I saw...

What I learned...

A laughable moment...

A surprising moment...

An unforeseeable moment...

My List
- ☐
- ☐
- ☐
- ☐
- ☐
- ☐
- ☐
- ☐
- ☐
- ☐

Snapped a selfie | Location...
Took a park sign selfie? - Y | N   The weather was ...

www.mynaturebookadventures.com

Plan Your Trip:

☐ Trip Plan Completed
☐ Day Trip   ☐ Overnight Stay
Reservations required: ☐ y ☐ n
Date reservations made: _____
Confirmation #: _____
Dog friendly?: ☐ y ☐ n

Places to stop and see along the way

Goals:

☐ _____
☐ _____
☐ _____
☐ _____
☐ _____
☐ _____

Destination Information:

Places we discovered along the way

Would you go again?: ☐ y ☐ n   Open all year?: ☐ y ☐ n

How I felt: 😊 🙂 😐 ☹️ 😢

☐ _____
☐ _____
☐ _____
☐ _____
☐ _____

Add your favorite ticket stub, postcard, photo, stamp, decals or drawings here

www.mynaturebookadventures.com

DESTINATION:

○ ○ ○ ○ ○ ○
S M T W T F S

Season Visited

_____
Star Rating
☆ ☆ ☆ ☆ ☆

My favorite souvenir... _____
My favorite thing about this place is... _____

Why I went ... _____
Who I went with ... _____
When I went ... _____

What I did... _____
What I saw... _____

What I learned... _____

A laughable moment... _____

A surprising moment... _____

An unforeseeable moment... _____

My List
☐ _____
☐ _____
☐ _____
☐ _____
☐ _____
☐ _____
☐ _____
☐ _____
☐ _____
☐ _____
☐ _____

Snapped a selfie | Location... _____
Took a park sign selfie? - Y | N   The weather was ...

www.mynaturebookadventures.com

Plan Your Trip:

☐ Trip Plan Completed
☐ Day Trip   ☐ Overnight Stay
Reservations required: ☐ y ☐ n
Date reservations made: _____
Confirmation #: _____
Dog friendly?: ☐ y ☐ n

Destination Information:

_____
_____

Places we discovered along the way

_____
_____
_____
_____

Places to stop and see along the way

_____
_____

Goals:

☐ _____
☐ _____
☐ _____
☐ _____
☐ _____
☐ _____

Would you go again?: ☐ y ☐ n   Open all year?: ☐ y ☐ n

How I felt: ☺ ☺ ☹ ☹

☐ _____
☐ _____
☐ _____
☐ _____
☐ _____

Add your favorite ticket stub, postcard, photo, stamp, decals or drawings here

www.mynaturebookadventures.com

DESTINATION:

S M T W T F S

Season Visited

Star Rating
☆☆☆☆☆

My favorite souvenir...
My favorite thing about this place is...

Why I went ...
Who I went with ...
When I went ...

What I did...
What I saw...

What I learned...

A laughable moment...

A surprising moment...

An unforeseeable moment...

My List
- ☐
- ☐
- ☐
- ☐
- ☐
- ☐
- ☐
- ☐
- ☐
- ☐
- ☐

Snapped a selfie | Location...

Took a park sign selfie? - Y | N   The weather was ...

www.mynaturebookadventures.com

Plan Your Trip:

☐ Trip Plan Completed
☐ Day Trip   ☐ Overnight Stay
Reservations required: ☐ y ☐ n
Date reservations made:
Confirmation #:
Dog friendly?: ☐ y ☐ n

Destination Information:

Places we discovered along the way

Places to stop and see along the way

Goals:

☐
☐
☐
☐
☐
☐

Would you go again?: ☐ y ☐ n   Open all year?: ☐ y ☐ n

How I felt: 😊 🙂 😐 🙁 😞

☐
☐
☐
☐
☐

Add your favorite ticket stub, postcard, photo, stamp, decals or drawings here

www.mynaturebookadventures.com

DESTINATION:

S M T W T F S

Season Visited

Star Rating

My favorite souvenir...
My favorite thing about this place is...

Why I went ...
Who I went with ...
When I went ...

What I did...
What I saw...

My List

What I learned...

A laughable moment...

A surprising moment...

An unforeseeable moment...

Snapped a selfie | Location...
Took a park sign selfie? - Y | N   The weather was ...

www.mynaturebookadventures.com

Plan Your Trip:

☐ Trip Plan Completed
☐ Day Trip   ☐ Overnight Stay
Reservations required: ☐ y ☐ n
Date reservations made: _____
Confirmation #: _____
Dog friendly?: ☐ y ☐ n

Destination Information:

_____
_____

Places we discovered along the way

_____
_____
_____
_____

Places to stop and see along the way

_____
_____

Goals:

☐ _____
☐ _____
☐ _____
☐ _____
☐ _____
☐ _____

Would you go again?: ☐ y ☐ n   Open all year?: ☐ y ☐ n

How I felt: ☺ ☺ ☺ ☹ ☹

☐ _____
☐ _____
☐ _____
☐ _____
☐ _____

Add your favorite ticket stub, postcard, photo, stamp, decals or drawings here

www.mynaturebookadventures.com

DESTINATION:

S M T W T F S

Season Visited

_____
Star Rating
☆☆☆☆☆

My favorite souvenir... _____
My favorite thing about this place is... _____

_____
Why I went ... _____
Who I went with ... _____
When I went ... _____

_____
What I did... _____
What I saw... _____

_____

What I learned... _____

My List
- ☐ _____
- ☐ _____
- ☐ _____
- ☐ _____
- ☐ _____
- ☐ _____
- ☐ _____
- ☐ _____
- ☐ _____
- ☐ _____
- ☐ _____
- ☐ _____

A laughable moment... _____

_____

A surprising moment... _____

_____

An unforeseeable moment... _____

_____

Snapped a selfie | Location... _____
Took a park sign selfie? - Y | N   The weather was ...

www.mynaturebookadventures.com

Plan Your Trip:

- ☐ Trip Plan Completed
- ☐ Day Trip   ☐ Overnight Stay

Reservations required: ☐ y ☐ n
Date reservations made: _____
Confirmation #: _____
Dog friendly?: ☐ y ☐ n

Destination Information:

Places we discovered along the way

Places to stop and see along the way

Goals:

- ☐ _____
- ☐ _____
- ☐ _____
- ☐ _____
- ☐ _____
- ☐ _____

Would you go again?: ☐ y ☐ n   Open all year?: ☐ y ☐ n

How I felt: ☺ ☺ ☹ ☹

- ☐ _____
- ☐ _____
- ☐ _____
- ☐ _____
- ☐ _____

Add your favorite ticket stub, postcard, photo, stamp, decals or drawings here

DESTINATION:

S M T W T F S

Season Visited

_____
Star Rating
☆☆☆☆☆

My favorite souvenir... _____
My favorite thing about this place is... _____
_____
Why I went ... _____
Who I went with ... _____
When I went ... _____

What I did... _____
What I saw... _____
_____

What I learned... _____
_____
_____
A laughable moment... _____
_____
_____
_____
A surprising moment... _____
_____
_____
_____
An unforeseeable moment... _____
_____
_____
_____

My List
- ☐ _____
- ☐ _____
- ☐ _____
- ☐ _____
- ☐ _____
- ☐ _____
- ☐ _____
- ☐ _____
- ☐ _____
- ☐ _____
- ☐ _____
- ☐ _____

Snapped a selfie | Location... _____
Took a park sign selfie? - Y | N   The weather was ...

www.mynaturebookadventures.com

Plan Your Trip:

☐ Trip Plan Completed
☐ Day Trip   ☐ Overnight Stay
Reservations required: ☐ y ☐ n
Date reservations made: _____
Confirmation #: _____
Dog friendly?: ☐ y ☐ n

Places to stop and see along the way

Goals:
☐ _____
☐ _____
☐ _____
☐ _____
☐ _____
☐ _____

Destination Information:

Places we discovered along the way

Would you go again?: ☐ y ☐ n   Open all year?: ☐ y ☐ n

How I felt: ☺ ☺ ☺ ☹ ☹

☐ _____
☐ _____
☐ _____
☐ _____
☐ _____

Add your favorite ticket stub, postcard, photo, stamp, decals or drawings here

www.mynaturebookadventures.com

DESTINATION:

S M T W T F S

Season Visited

Star Rating

My favorite souvenir...
My favorite thing about this place is...

Why I went ...
Who I went with ...
When I went ...

What I did...
What I saw...

My List

What I learned...

A laughable moment...

A surprising moment...

An unforeseeable moment...

Snapped a selfie | Location...

Took a park sign selfie? - Y | N   The weather was ...

www.mynaturebookadventures.com

Plan Your Trip:

☐ Trip Plan Completed
☐ Day Trip   ☐ Overnight Stay
Reservations required: ☐ y ☐ n
Date reservations made: _____
Confirmation #: _____
Dog friendly?: ☐ y ☐ n

Places to stop and see along the way

Goals:
☐ _____
☐ _____
☐ _____
☐ _____
☐ _____
☐ _____

Destination Information:

Places we discovered along the way

Would you go again?: ☐ y ☐ n   Open all year?: ☐ y ☐ n

How I felt: 😊 🙂 😐 ☹️ 😞

☐ _____
☐ _____
☐ _____
☐ _____
☐ _____

Add your favorite ticket stub, postcard, photo, stamp, decals or drawings here

www.mynaturebookadventures.com

DESTINATION:

S M T W T F S

Season Visited

_____
Star Rating
☆☆☆☆☆

My favorite souvenir... _____
My favorite thing about this place is... _____
_____
Why I went ... _____
Who I went with ... _____
When I went ... _____

What I did... _____
What I saw... _____

_____
What I learned... _____
_____

A laughable moment... _____
_____
_____

A surprising moment... _____
_____
_____

An unforeseeable moment... _____
_____
_____

My List
☐ _____
☐ _____
☐ _____
☐ _____
☐ _____
☐ _____
☐ _____
☐ _____
☐ _____
☐ _____
☐ _____

Snapped a selfie | Location... _____
Took a park sign selfie? - y | n   The weather was ...

www.mynaturebookadventures.com

Plan Your Trip:

☐ Trip Plan Completed
☐ Day Trip   ☐ Overnight Stay
Reservations required: ☐ y ☐ n
Date reservations made: _____
Confirmation #: _____
Dog friendly?: ☐ y ☐ n

Destination Information:

_____
_____

Places we discovered along the way
_____
_____
_____

Places to stop and see along the way
_____
_____

Goals:

☐ _____
☐ _____
☐ _____
☐ _____
☐ _____
☐ _____

Would you go again?: ☐ y ☐ n   Open all year?: ☐ y ☐ n

How I felt: 😊 🙂 😐 🙁 ☹️

☐ _____
☐ _____
☐ _____
☐ _____
☐ _____

Add your favorite ticket stub, postcard, photo, stamp, decals or drawings here

www.mynaturebookadventures.com

Destination:

S M T W T F S

Season Visited

Star Rating

My favorite souvenir...
My favorite thing about this place is...

Why I went ...
Who I went with ...
When I went ...

What I did...
What I saw...

What I learned...

A laughable moment...

A surprising moment...

An unforeseeable moment...

My List
-
-
-
-
-
-
-
-
-
-
-
-

Snapped a selfie | Location...
Took a park sign selfie? - Y | N   The weather was ...

www.mynaturebookadventures.com

Plan Your Trip:

- ☐ Trip Plan Completed
- ☐ Day Trip   ☐ Overnight Stay

Reservations required: ☐ y ☐ n
Date reservations made: _____
Confirmation #: _____
Dog friendly?: ☐ y ☐ n

Destination Information:

_____
_____

Places we discovered along the way

_____
_____
_____

Places to stop and see along the way

_____
_____

Goals:

Would you go again?: ☐ y ☐ n   Open all year?: ☐ y ☐ n

How I felt: 😊 🙂 😐 🙁 😞

- ☐ _____
- ☐ _____
- ☐ _____
- ☐ _____
- ☐ _____
- ☐ _____

- ☐ _____
- ☐ _____
- ☐ _____
- ☐ _____
- ☐ _____

Add your favorite ticket stub, postcard, photo, stamp, decals or drawings here

www.mynaturebookadventures.com

DESTINATION:

S M T W T F S

Season Visited

Star Rating

My favorite souvenir... _____
My favorite thing about this place is... _____

_____

Why I went ... _____
Who I went with ... _____
When I went ... _____

_____

What I did... _____
What I saw... _____

_____

What I learned... _____

_____

A laughable moment... _____

_____

_____

A surprising moment... _____

_____

_____

An unforeseeable moment... _____

_____

_____

My List
- ☐ _____
- ☐ _____
- ☐ _____
- ☐ _____
- ☐ _____
- ☐ _____
- ☐ _____
- ☐ _____
- ☐ _____
- ☐ _____
- ☐ _____
- ☐ _____

Snapped a selfie | Location... _____
Took a park sign selfie? - Y | N   The weather was ...

www.mynaturebookadventures.com

Plan Your Trip:

☐ Trip Plan Completed
☐ Day Trip   ☐ Overnight Stay
Reservations required: ☐ y ☐ n
Date reservations made: _____
Confirmation #: _____
Dog friendly?: ☐ y ☐ n

Destination Information:

_____

Places we discovered along the way

_____
_____
_____
_____

Places to stop and see along the way

_____
_____

Goals:

Would you go again?: ☐ y ☐ n   Open all year?: ☐ y ☐ n

How I felt: ☺ ☺ ☺ ☹ ☹

☐ _____
☐ _____   ☐ _____
☐ _____   ☐ _____
☐ _____   ☐ _____
☐ _____   ☐ _____
☐ _____   ☐ _____

Add your favorite ticket stub, postcard, photo, stamp, decals or drawings here

www.mynaturebookadventures.com

DESTINATION:

S M T W T F S

Season Visited

Star Rating
☆☆☆☆☆

My favorite souvenir... _____

My favorite thing about this place is... _____

Why I went ... _____

Who I went with ... _____

When I went ... _____

What I did... _____

What I saw... _____

What I learned... _____

A laughable moment... _____

A surprising moment... _____

An unforeseeable moment... _____

My List
- ☐ _____
- ☐ _____
- ☐ _____
- ☐ _____
- ☐ _____
- ☐ _____
- ☐ _____
- ☐ _____
- ☐ _____
- ☐ _____
- ☐ _____

Snapped a selfie | Location... _____

Took a park sign selfie? - y | n   The weather was ...

www.mynaturebookadventures.com

Plan Your Trip:

☐ Trip Plan Completed
☐ Day Trip   ☐ Overnight Stay
Reservations required: ☐ y ☐ n
Date reservations made: _____
Confirmation #: _____
Dog friendly?: ☐ y ☐ n

Destination Information:

Places we discovered along the way

Places to stop and see along the way

Goals:

☐ _____
☐ _____
☐ _____
☐ _____
☐ _____
☐ _____

Would you go again?: ☐ y ☐ n   Open all year?: ☐ y ☐ n

How I felt: ☺ ☺ ☺ ☹ ☹

☐ _____
☐ _____
☐ _____
☐ _____
☐ _____

Add your favorite ticket stub, postcard, photo, stamp, decals or drawings here

www.mynaturebookadventures.com

DESTINATION:

S M T W T F S

Season Visited

Star Rating
☆☆☆☆☆

My favorite souvenir...
My favorite thing about this place is...

Why I went ...
Who I went with ...
When I went ...

What I did...
What I saw...

What I learned...

A laughable moment...

A surprising moment...

An unforeseeable moment...

My List
- ☐
- ☐
- ☐
- ☐
- ☐
- ☐
- ☐
- ☐
- ☐
- ☐
- ☐

Snapped a selfie | Location...
Took a park sign selfie? - Y | N   The weather was ...

www.mynaturebookadventures.com

Plan Your Trip:

☐ Trip Plan Completed
☐ Day Trip   ☐ Overnight Stay
Reservations required: ☐ y ☐ n
Date reservations made:
Confirmation #:
Dog friendly?: ☐ y ☐ n

Destination Information:

Places we discovered along the way

Places to stop and see along the way

Goals:

☐
☐
☐
☐
☐
☐

Would you go again?: ☐ y ☐ n   Open all year?: ☐ y ☐ n

How I felt: ☺ ☺ ☺ ☹ ☹

☐
☐
☐
☐
☐

Add your favorite ticket stub, postcard, photo, stamp, decals or drawings here

www.mynaturebookadventures.com

DESTINATION:

S M T W T F S

Season Visited

Star Rating
☆☆☆☆☆

My favorite souvenir...
My favorite thing about this place is...

Why I went ...
Who I went with ...
When I went ...

What I did...
What I saw...

What I learned...

A laughable moment...

A surprising moment...

An unforeseeable moment...

My List
- ☐
- ☐
- ☐
- ☐
- ☐
- ☐
- ☐
- ☐
- ☐
- ☐
- ☐

Snapped a selfie | Location...

Took a park sign selfie? - Y | N   The weather was ...

www.mynaturebookadventures.com

Plan Your Trip:

☐ Trip Plan Completed
☐ Day Trip   ☐ Overnight Stay
Reservations required: ☐ y ☐ n
Date reservations made: _____
Confirmation #: _____
Dog friendly?: ☐ y ☐ n

Destination Information:

Places we discovered along the way

Places to stop and see along the way

Goals:

☐ _____
☐ _____
☐ _____
☐ _____
☐ _____
☐ _____

Would you go again?: ☐ y ☐ n   Open all year?: ☐ y ☐ n

How I felt: 😊 🙂 😐 🙁 ☹️

☐ _____
☐ _____
☐ _____
☐ _____

Add your favorite ticket stub, postcard, photo, stamp, decals or drawings here

www.mynaturebookadventures.com

DESTINATION:

S M T W T F S

Season Visited

_____
Star Rating
☆ ☆ ☆ ☆ ☆

My favorite souvenir... _____

My favorite thing about this place is... _____

_____

Why I went ... _____

Who I went with ... _____

When I went ... _____

_____

What I did... _____

What I saw... _____

_____

My List
- ☐ _____
- ☐ _____
- ☐ _____
- ☐ _____
- ☐ _____
- ☐ _____
- ☐ _____
- ☐ _____
- ☐ _____
- ☐ _____
- ☐ _____
- ☐ _____

What I learned... _____

_____

_____

A laughable moment... _____

_____

_____

_____

A surprising moment... _____

_____

_____

_____

An unforeseeable moment... _____

_____

_____

_____

📷 Snapped a selfie | Location... _____

📷 Took a park sign selfie? - Y | N   The weather was ...

www.mynaturebookadventures.com

Plan Your Trip:

- ☐ Trip Plan Completed
- ☐ Day Trip   ☐ Overnight Stay

Reservations required: ☐ y ☐ n
Date reservations made: _____
Confirmation #: _____
Dog friendly?: ☐ y ☐ n

Destination Information:

_____

Places we discovered along the way

_____
_____
_____

Places to stop and see along the way

_____
_____

Goals:

- ☐ _____
- ☐ _____
- ☐ _____
- ☐ _____
- ☐ _____
- ☐ _____

Would you go again?: ☐ y ☐ n   Open all year?: ☐ y ☐ n

How I felt: ☺ ☺ ☺ ☹ ☹

- ☐ _____
- ☐ _____
- ☐ _____
- ☐ _____
- ☐ _____

Add your favorite ticket stub, postcard, photo, stamp, decals or drawings here

www.mynaturebookadventures.com

DESTINATION:		S M T W T F S

Season Visited

Star Rating
☆☆☆☆☆

My favorite souvenir...
My favorite thing about this place is...

Why I went ...
Who I went with ...
When I went ...

What I did...
What I saw...

What I learned...

A laughable moment...

A surprising moment...

An unforeseeable moment...

My List
- ☐
- ☐
- ☐
- ☐
- ☐
- ☐
- ☐
- ☐
- ☐
- ☐
- ☐

Snapped a selfie | Location...
Took a park sign selfie? - Y | N   The weather was ...

www.mynaturebookadventures.com

Plan Your Trip:

☐ Trip Plan Completed
☐ Day Trip   ☐ Overnight Stay
Reservations required: ☐ y ☐ n
Date reservations made:
Confirmation #:
Dog friendly?: ☐ y ☐ n

Destination Information:

Places we discovered along the way

Places to stop and see along the way

Goals:

☐
☐
☐
☐
☐
☐

Would you go again?: ☐ y ☐ n   Open all year?: ☐ y ☐ n

How I felt: ☺ ☺ ☺ ☹ ☹

☐
☐
☐
☐

Add your favorite ticket stub, postcard, photo, stamp, decals or drawings here

www.mynaturebookadventures.com

DESTINATION:

S M T W T F S

Season Visited

_____
Star Rating
☆☆☆☆☆

My favorite souvenir... _____
My favorite thing about this place is... _____

Why I went ... _____
Who I went with ... _____
When I went ... _____

What I did... _____
What I saw... _____

What I learned... _____

My List
☐ _____
☐ _____
☐ _____
☐ _____
☐ _____
☐ _____
☐ _____
☐ _____
☐ _____
☐ _____
☐ _____
☐ _____

A laughable moment... _____

A surprising moment... _____

An unforeseeable moment... _____

Snapped a selfie | Location... _____
Took a park sign selfie? - Y | N   The weather was ...

www.mynaturebookadventures.com

Plan Your Trip:

☐ Trip Plan Completed
☐ Day Trip   ☐ Overnight Stay
Reservations required: ☐ y ☐ n
Date reservations made: _____
Confirmation #: _____
Dog friendly?: ☐ y ☐ n

Destination Information:

Places we discovered along the way

Places to stop and see along the way

Goals:

☐ _____
☐ _____
☐ _____
☐ _____
☐ _____
☐ _____

Would you go again?: ☐ y ☐ n   Open all year?: ☐ y ☐ n

How I felt: 😊😐☹️😞

☐ _____
☐ _____
☐ _____
☐ _____
☐ _____

Add your favorite ticket stub, postcard, photo, stamp, decals or drawings here

www.mynaturebookadventures.com

DESTINATION:

S M T W T F S

Season Visited

My favorite souvenir... _____

My favorite thing about this place is... _____

Star Rating
☆☆☆☆☆

Why I went ... _____
Who I went with ... _____
When I went ... _____

What I did... _____
What I saw... _____

My List
☐ _____
☐ _____
☐ _____
☐ _____
☐ _____
☐ _____
☐ _____
☐ _____
☐ _____
☐ _____
☐ _____
☐ _____

What I learned... _____

A laughable moment... _____

A surprising moment... _____

An unforeseeable moment... _____

📷 Snapped a selfie | Location... _____
📷 Took a park sign selfie? - Y | N

The weather was ...

www.mynaturebookadventures.com

Plan Your Trip:

☐ Trip Plan Completed
☐ Day Trip   ☐ Overnight Stay
Reservations required: ☐ y ☐ n
Date reservations made: _____
Confirmation #: _____
Dog friendly?: ☐ y ☐ n

Destination Information:

_____
_____

Places we discovered along the way

_____
_____
_____

Places to stop and see along the way

_____
_____

Goals:

Would you go again?: ☐ y ☐ n   Open all year?: ☐ y ☐ n

How I felt: 😊 🙂 😐 🙁 😞

☐ _____
☐ _____
☐ _____
☐ _____
☐ _____
☐ _____

☐ _____
☐ _____
☐ _____
☐ _____
☐ _____

Add your favorite ticket stub, postcard, photo, stamp, decals or drawings here

DESTINATION:

S M T W T F S

Season Visited

_____
Star Rating
☆☆☆☆☆

My favorite souvenir... _____

My favorite thing about this place is... _____

Why I went ... _____

Who I went with ... _____

When I went ... _____

What I did... _____

What I saw... _____

What I learned... _____

A laughable moment... _____

A surprising moment... _____

An unforeseeable moment... _____

My List
- ☐ _____
- ☐ _____
- ☐ _____
- ☐ _____
- ☐ _____
- ☐ _____
- ☐ _____
- ☐ _____
- ☐ _____
- ☐ _____
- ☐ _____
- ☐ _____

Snapped a selfie | Location... _____

Took a park sign selfie? - Y | N

The weather was ...

www.mynaturebookadventures.com

Plan Your Trip:

☐ Trip Plan Completed
☐ Day Trip ☐ Overnight Stay
Reservations required: ☐ y ☐ n
Date reservations made: _____
Confirmation #: _____
Dog friendly?: ☐ y ☐ n

Places to stop and see along the way

Goals:
☐ _____
☐ _____
☐ _____
☐ _____
☐ _____
☐ _____

Destination Information:

Places we discovered along the way

Would you go again?: ☐ y ☐ n   Open all year?: ☐ y ☐ n

How I felt: 😊 🙂 😐 ☹️ 😟

☐ _____
☐ _____
☐ _____
☐ _____
☐ _____

Add your favorite ticket stub, postcard, photo, stamp, decals or drawings here

www.mynaturebookadventures.com

DESTINATION:

S M T W T F S

Season Visited

Star Rating
☆☆☆☆☆

My favorite souvenir... _____

My favorite thing about this place is... _____

Why I went ... _____

Who I went with ... _____

When I went ... _____

What I did... _____

What I saw... _____

What I learned... _____

A laughable moment... _____

A surprising moment... _____

An unforeseeable moment... _____

My List
- ☐ _____
- ☐ _____
- ☐ _____
- ☐ _____
- ☐ _____
- ☐ _____
- ☐ _____
- ☐ _____
- ☐ _____
- ☐ _____
- ☐ _____
- ☐ _____

Snapped a selfie | Location... _____

Took a park sign selfie? - Y | N

The weather was ...

www.mynaturebookadventures.com

Plan Your Trip:

☐ Trip Plan Completed
☐ Day Trip   ☐ Overnight Stay
Reservations required: ☐ y ☐ n
Date reservations made: _____
Confirmation #: _____
Dog friendly?: ☐ y ☐ n

Destination Information:

_____
_____

Places we discovered along the way
_____
_____
_____

Places to stop and see along the way
_____
_____

Goals:

☐ _____
☐ _____
☐ _____
☐ _____
☐ _____
☐ _____

Would you go again?: ☐ y ☐ n   Open all year?: ☐ y ☐ n

How I felt: ☺ ☺ ☺ ☹ ☹

☐ _____
☐ _____
☐ _____
☐ _____
☐ _____

Add your favorite ticket stub, postcard, photo, stamp, decals or drawings here

www.mynaturebookadventures.com

DESTINATION:

S M T W T F S

Season Visited

Star Rating

My favorite souvenir...
My favorite thing about this place is...

Why I went ...
Who I went with ...
When I went ...

What I did...
What I saw...

What I learned...

My List

A laughable moment...

A surprising moment...

An unforeseeable moment...

Snapped a selfie | Location...

Took a park sign selfie? - Y | N   The weather was ...

www.mynaturebookadventures.com

Plan Your Trip:

- ☐ Trip Plan Completed
- ☐ Day Trip   ☐ Overnight Stay

Reservations required: ☐ y ☐ n
Date reservations made: _____
Confirmation #: _____
Dog friendly?: ☐ y ☐ n

Destination Information:

_____

Places we discovered along the way

_____

Places to stop and see along the way

_____

Goals:

- ☐ _____
- ☐ _____
- ☐ _____
- ☐ _____
- ☐ _____
- ☐ _____

Would you go again?: ☐ y ☐ n   Open all year?: ☐ y ☐ n

How I felt: 😊 🙂 😐 ☹️ 😞

- ☐ _____
- ☐ _____
- ☐ _____
- ☐ _____
- ☐ _____

Add your favorite ticket stub, postcard, photo, stamp, decals or drawings here

www.mynaturebookadventures.com

DESTINATION:

S M T W T F S

Season Visited

_____
Star Rating
☆ ☆ ☆ ☆ ☆

My favorite souvenir... _____

My favorite thing about this place is... _____

Why I went ... _____

Who I went with ... _____

When I went ... _____

What I did... _____

What I saw... _____

What I learned... _____

A laughable moment... _____

A surprising moment... _____

An unforeseeable moment... _____

My List
- ☐ _____
- ☐ _____
- ☐ _____
- ☐ _____
- ☐ _____
- ☐ _____
- ☐ _____
- ☐ _____
- ☐ _____
- ☐ _____
- ☐ _____
- ☐ _____

Snapped a selfie | Location... _____

Took a park sign selfie? - Y | N   The weather was ...

www.mynaturebookadventures.com

Plan Your Trip:

- ☐ Trip Plan Completed
- ☐ Day Trip   ☐ Overnight Stay

Reservations required: ☐ y ☐ n
Date reservations made: _____
Confirmation #: _____
Dog friendly?: ☐ y ☐ n

Destination Information:

Places we discovered along the way

Places to stop and see along the way

Goals:

- ☐ _____
- ☐ _____
- ☐ _____
- ☐ _____
- ☐ _____
- ☐ _____

Would you go again?: ☐ y ☐ n   Open all year?: ☐ y ☐ n

How I felt: 😊🙂☹️😣

- ☐ _____
- ☐ _____
- ☐ _____
- ☐ _____

Add your favorite ticket stub, postcard, photo, stamp, decals or drawings here

www.mynaturebookadventures.com

DESTINATION:

S M T W T F S

Season Visited

_____
Star Rating
☆☆☆☆☆

My favorite souvenir... _____

My favorite thing about this place is... _____

_____

Why I went ... _____

Who I went with ... _____

When I went ... _____

_____

What I did... _____

What I saw... _____

_____

_____

My List

☐ _____
☐ _____
☐ _____
☐ _____
☐ _____
☐ _____
☐ _____
☐ _____
☐ _____
☐ _____
☐ _____
☐ _____

What I learned... _____

_____

A laughable moment... _____

_____

_____

_____

A surprising moment... _____

_____

_____

_____

An unforeseeable moment... _____

_____

_____

_____

📷 Snapped a selfie | Location... _____

📷 Took a park sign selfie? - Y | N   The weather was ...

www.mynaturebookadventures.com

Plan Your Trip:

☐ Trip Plan Completed
☐ Day Trip   ☐ Overnight Stay
Reservations required: ☐ y ☐ n
Date reservations made: _____
Confirmation #: _____
Dog friendly?: ☐ y ☐ n

Destination Information:

Places we discovered along the way

Places to stop and see along the way

Goals:

☐ _____
☐ _____
☐ _____
☐ _____
☐ _____
☐ _____

Would you go again?: ☐ y ☐ n   Open all year?: ☐ y ☐ n

How I felt: 😊 🙂 😐 ☹️ 😞

☐ _____
☐ _____
☐ _____
☐ _____
☐ _____

Add your favorite ticket stub, postcard, photo, stamp, decals or drawings here

www.mynaturebookadventures.com

DESTINATION:

S M T W T F S

Season Visited

_____
Star Rating

My favorite souvenir... _____
My favorite thing about this place is... _____

Why I went ... _____
Who I went with ... _____
When I went ... _____

What I did... _____
What I saw... _____

What I learned... _____

A laughable moment... _____

A surprising moment... _____

An unforeseeable moment... _____

My List
- ☐ _____
- ☐ _____
- ☐ _____
- ☐ _____
- ☐ _____
- ☐ _____
- ☐ _____
- ☐ _____
- ☐ _____
- ☐ _____
- ☐ _____

Snapped a selfie | Location... _____
Took a park sign selfie? - Y | N   The weather was ...

www.mynaturebookadventures.com

Plan Your Trip:

Destination Information:

☐ Trip Plan Completed
☐ Day Trip   ☐ Overnight Stay
Reservations required: ☐ y ☐ n
Date reservations made: _____
Confirmation #: _____
Dog friendly?: ☐ y ☐ n

Places we discovered along the way

Places to stop and see along the way

Goals:

Would you go again?: ☐ y ☐ n   Open all year?: ☐ y ☐ n

How I felt: 😊😊😐☹️☹️

☐ _____
☐ _____
☐ _____
☐ _____
☐ _____
☐ _____

☐ _____
☐ _____
☐ _____
☐ _____

Add your favorite ticket stub, postcard, photo, stamp, decals or drawings here

www.mynaturebookadventures.com

DESTINATION:

S M T W T F S

Season Visited

_____
Star Rating
☆☆☆☆☆

My favorite souvenir...
My favorite thing about this place is...

Why I went ...
Who I went with ...
When I went ...

What I did...
What I saw...

What I learned...

A laughable moment...

A surprising moment...

An unforeseeable moment...

My List
- [ ]
- [ ]
- [ ]
- [ ]
- [ ]
- [ ]
- [ ]
- [ ]
- [ ]
- [ ]
- [ ]
- [ ]

📷 Snapped a selfie | Location...
📷 Took a park sign selfie? - Y | N   The weather was ...

www.mynaturebookadventures.com

Plan Your Trip:

☐ Trip Plan Completed
☐ Day Trip   ☐ Overnight Stay
Reservations required: ☐ y ☐ n
Date reservations made: _____
Confirmation #: _____
Dog friendly?: ☐ y ☐ n

Destination Information:

Places we discovered along the way

Places to stop and see along the way

Goals:

☐ _____
☐ _____
☐ _____
☐ _____
☐ _____
☐ _____

Would you go again?: ☐ y ☐ n   Open all year?: ☐ y ☐ n

How I felt: ☺ ☺ ☺ ☹ ☹

☐ _____
☐ _____
☐ _____
☐ _____

Add your favorite ticket stub, postcard, photo, stamp, decals or drawings here

www.mynaturebookadventures.com

DESTINATION:

S M T W T F S

Season Visited

_____
Star Rating
☆☆☆☆☆

My favorite souvenir... _____
My favorite thing about this place is... _____

Why I went ... _____
Who I went with ... _____
When I went ... _____

What I did... _____
What I saw... _____

What I learned... _____

A laughable moment... _____

A surprising moment... _____

An unforeseeable moment... _____

My List
- ☐ _____
- ☐ _____
- ☐ _____
- ☐ _____
- ☐ _____
- ☐ _____
- ☐ _____
- ☐ _____
- ☐ _____
- ☐ _____
- ☐ _____
- ☐ _____

📷 Snapped a selfie | Location... _____
📷 Took a park sign selfie? - Y | N   The weather was ...

www.mynaturebookadventures.com

Plan Your Trip:

☐ Trip Plan Completed
☐ Day Trip   ☐ Overnight Stay
Reservations required: ☐ y ☐ n
Date reservations made: _____
Confirmation #: _____
Dog friendly?: ☐ y ☐ n

Destination Information:

_____
_____

Places we discovered along the way

_____
_____
_____

Places to stop and see along the way

_____
_____

Goals:

☐ _____
☐ _____
☐ _____
☐ _____
☐ _____
☐ _____

Would you go again?: ☐ y ☐ n   Open all year?: ☐ y ☐ n

How I felt: 😊 🙂 😐 ☹️ 😞

☐ _____
☐ _____
☐ _____
☐ _____
☐ _____

Add your favorite ticket stub, postcard, photo, stamp, decals or drawings here

www.mynaturebookadventures.com

DESTINATION:

S M T W T F S

Season Visited

_____
Star Rating
☆☆☆☆☆

My favorite souvenir... _____
My favorite thing about this place is... _____
_____
Why I went ... _____
Who I went with ... _____
When I went ... _____
_____
What I did... _____
What I saw... _____

My List
- ☐ _____
- ☐ _____
- ☐ _____
- ☐ _____
- ☐ _____
- ☐ _____
- ☐ _____
- ☐ _____
- ☐ _____
- ☐ _____
- ☐ _____

What I learned... _____
_____
_____
A laughable moment... _____
_____
_____
_____
A surprising moment... _____
_____
_____
_____
An unforeseeable moment... _____
_____
_____
_____

Snapped a selfie | Location... _____
Took a park sign selfie? - Y | N   The weather was ...

www.mynaturebookadventures.com

Plan Your Trip:

☐ Trip Plan Completed
☐ Day Trip   ☐ Overnight Stay
Reservations required: ☐ y ☐ n
Date reservations made: _____
Confirmation #: _____
Dog friendly?: ☐ y ☐ n

Destination Information:

_____
_____

Places we discovered along the way

_____
_____
_____

Places to stop and see along the way

_____
_____

Goals:

☐ _____
☐ _____
☐ _____
☐ _____
☐ _____
☐ _____

Would you go again?: ☐ y ☐ n   Open all year?: ☐ y ☐ n

How I felt: ☺ ☺ ☺ ☹ ☹

☐ _____
☐ _____
☐ _____
☐ _____
☐ _____

Add your favorite ticket stub, postcard, photo, stamp, decals or drawings here

www.mynaturebookadventures.com

DESTINATION:

S M T W T F S

Season Visited

Star Rating
☆☆☆☆☆

My favorite souvenir... _____

My favorite thing about this place is... _____

_____

Why I went ... _____

Who I went with ... _____

When I went ... _____

_____

What I did... _____

What I saw... _____

_____

My List
- ☐ _____
- ☐ _____
- ☐ _____
- ☐ _____
- ☐ _____
- ☐ _____
- ☐ _____
- ☐ _____
- ☐ _____
- ☐ _____
- ☐ _____
- ☐ _____

What I learned... _____

_____

A laughable moment... _____

_____

_____

A surprising moment... _____

_____

_____

An unforeseeable moment... _____

_____

_____

Snapped a selfie | Location... _____

Took a park sign selfie? - Y | N   The weather was ...

www.mynaturebookadventures.com

Plan Your Trip:

- ☐ Trip Plan Completed
- ☐ Day Trip   ☐ Overnight Stay

Reservations required: ☐ y ☐ n
Date reservations made: _____
Confirmation #: _____
Dog friendly?: ☐ y ☐ n

Goals:
- ☐ _____
- ☐ _____
- ☐ _____
- ☐ _____
- ☐ _____
- ☐ _____

Destination Information:

Places we discovered along the way

Places to stop and see along the way

Would you go again?: ☐ y ☐ n   Open all year?: ☐ y ☐ n

How I felt: ☺ ☺ ☺ ☹ ☹

- ☐ _____
- ☐ _____
- ☐ _____
- ☐ _____

Add your favorite ticket stub, postcard, photo, stamp, decals or drawings here

www.mynaturebookadventures.com

DESTINATION:

S M T W T F S

Season Visited

_____
Star Rating
☆ ☆ ☆ ☆ ☆

My favorite souvenir...
My favorite thing about this place is...

Why I went ...
Who I went with ...
When I went ...

What I did...
What I saw...

What I learned...

My List
- ☐ _____
- ☐ _____
- ☐ _____
- ☐ _____
- ☐ _____
- ☐ _____
- ☐ _____
- ☐ _____
- ☐ _____
- ☐ _____
- ☐ _____
- ☐ _____

A laughable moment...

A surprising moment...

An unforeseeable moment...

Snapped a selfie | Location...
Took a park sign selfie? - y | n   The weather was ...

www.mynaturebookadventures.com

Plan Your Trip:

- ☐ Trip Plan Completed
- ☐ Day Trip   ☐ Overnight Stay

Reservations required: ☐ y ☐ n
Date reservations made: _____
Confirmation #: _____
Dog friendly?: ☐ y ☐ n

Destination Information:

Places we discovered along the way

Places to stop and see along the way

Goals:

- ☐ _____
- ☐ _____
- ☐ _____
- ☐ _____
- ☐ _____
- ☐ _____

Would you go again?: ☐ y ☐ n   Open all year?: ☐ y ☐ n

How I felt: 😊 🙂 😐 ☹️ 😢

- ☐ _____
- ☐ _____
- ☐ _____
- ☐ _____

Add your favorite ticket stub, postcard, photo, stamp, decals or drawings here

www.mynaturebookadventures.com

DESTINATION:

S M T W T F S

Season Visited

_____
Star Rating
☆☆☆☆☆

My favorite souvenir...
My favorite thing about this place is...

Why I went ...
Who I went with ...
When I went ...

What I did...
What I saw...

What I learned...

A laughable moment...

A surprising moment...

An unforeseeable moment...

My List
- ☐ _____
- ☐ _____
- ☐ _____
- ☐ _____
- ☐ _____
- ☐ _____
- ☐ _____
- ☐ _____
- ☐ _____
- ☐ _____
- ☐ _____
- ☐ _____

Snapped a selfie | Location...
Took a park sign selfie? - Y | N   The weather was ...

www.mynaturebookadventures.com

Plan Your Trip:

- ☐ Trip Plan Completed
- ☐ Day Trip ☐ Overnight Stay

Reservations required: ☐ y ☐ n
Date reservations made:
Confirmation #:
Dog friendly?: ☐ y ☐ n

Destination Information:

Places we discovered along the way

Places to stop and see along the way

Goals:

- ☐
- ☐
- ☐
- ☐
- ☐
- ☐

Would you go again?: ☐ y ☐ n   Open all year?: ☐ y ☐ n

How I felt: 😊 🙂 😐 🙁 ☹️

- ☐
- ☐
- ☐
- ☐

Add your favorite ticket stub, postcard, photo, stamp, decals or drawings here

www.mynaturebookadventures.com

DESTINATION:

S M T W T F S

Season Visited

Star Rating

My favorite souvenir...
My favorite thing about this place is...

Why I went ...
Who I went with ...
When I went ...

What I did...
What I saw...

What I learned...

My List

A laughable moment...

A surprising moment...

An unforeseeable moment...

Snapped a selfie | Location...

Took a park sign selfie? - Y | N   The weather was ...

www.mynaturebookadventures.com

Plan Your Trip:

☐ Trip Plan Completed
☐ Day Trip   ☐ Overnight Stay
Reservations required: ☐ y ☐ n
Date reservations made: _____
Confirmation #: _____
Dog friendly?: ☐ y ☐ n

Destination Information:

Places we discovered along the way

Places to stop and see along the way

Goals:

☐ _____
☐ _____
☐ _____
☐ _____
☐ _____
☐ _____

Would you go again?: ☐ y ☐ n   Open all year?: ☐ y ☐ n

How I felt: ☺ ☺ ☺ ☹ ☹

☐ _____
☐ _____
☐ _____
☐ _____
☐ _____

Add your favorite ticket stub, postcard, photo, stamp, decals or drawings here

www.mynaturebookadventures.com

DESTINATION:

○ ○ ○ ○ ○ ○ ○
S M T W T F S

Season Visited

Star Rating
☆ ☆ ☆ ☆ ☆

My favorite souvenir... _____

My favorite thing about this place is... _____

Why I went ... _____

Who I went with ... _____

When I went ... _____

What I did... _____

What I saw... _____

What I learned... _____

A laughable moment... _____

A surprising moment... _____

An unforeseeable moment... _____

My List
- ☐ _____
- ☐ _____
- ☐ _____
- ☐ _____
- ☐ _____
- ☐ _____
- ☐ _____
- ☐ _____
- ☐ _____
- ☐ _____
- ☐ _____
- ☐ _____

Snapped a selfie | Location... _____

Took a park sign selfie? - y | n

The weather was ...

www.mynaturebookadventures.com

Plan Your Trip:

☐ Trip Plan Completed
☐ Day Trip   ☐ Overnight Stay
Reservations required: ☐ y ☐ n
Date reservations made: _____
Confirmation #: _____
Dog friendly?: ☐ y ☐ n

Destination Information:

Places we discovered along the way

Places to stop and see along the way

Goals:

☐ _____
☐ _____
☐ _____
☐ _____
☐ _____
☐ _____

Would you go again?: ☐ y ☐ n   Open all year?: ☐ y ☐ n

How I felt: ☺ ☺ ☹ ☹

☐ _____
☐ _____
☐ _____
☐ _____
☐ _____

Add your favorite ticket stub, postcard, photo, stamp, decals or drawings here

www.mynaturebookadventures.com

DESTINATION:

S M T W T F S

Season Visited

_____
Star Rating
☆☆☆☆☆

My favorite souvenir... _____

My favorite thing about this place is... _____

_____

Why I went ... _____

Who I went with ... _____

When I went ... _____

_____

What I did... _____

What I saw... _____

_____

My List
- ☐ _____
- ☐ _____
- ☐ _____
- ☐ _____
- ☐ _____
- ☐ _____
- ☐ _____
- ☐ _____
- ☐ _____
- ☐ _____
- ☐ _____

What I learned... _____

_____

A laughable moment... _____

_____

_____

A surprising moment... _____

_____

_____

An unforeseeable moment... _____

_____

_____

Snapped a selfie | Location... _____

Took a park sign selfie? - Y | N   The weather was ...

www.mynaturebookadventures.com

Plan Your Trip:

☐ Trip Plan Completed
☐ Day Trip   ☐ Overnight Stay
Reservations required: ☐ y ☐ n
Date reservations made: _____
Confirmation #: _____
Dog friendly?: ☐ y ☐ n

Destination Information:

Places we discovered along the way

Places to stop and see along the way

Goals:

☐ _____
☐ _____
☐ _____
☐ _____
☐ _____
☐ _____

Would you go again?: ☐ y ☐ n   Open all year?: ☐ y ☐ n

How I felt: 😊😊😐☹️😣

☐ _____
☐ _____
☐ _____
☐ _____
☐ _____

Add your favorite ticket stub, postcard, photo, stamp, decals or drawings here

www.mynaturebookadventures.com

DESTINATION:

S M T W T F S

Season Visited

Star Rating
☆☆☆☆☆

My favorite souvenir...
My favorite thing about this place is...

Why I went ...
Who I went with ...
When I went ...

What I did...
What I saw...

What I learned...

A laughable moment...

A surprising moment...

An unforeseeable moment...

My List
- ☐
- ☐
- ☐
- ☐
- ☐
- ☐
- ☐
- ☐
- ☐
- ☐
- ☐

Snapped a selfie | Location...

Took a park sign selfie? - y | n   The weather was ...

www.mynaturebookadventures.com

Plan Your Trip:

☐ Trip Plan Completed
☐ Day Trip   ☐ Overnight Stay
Reservations required: ☐ y ☐ n
Date reservations made: _____
Confirmation #: _____
Dog friendly?: ☐ y ☐ n

Destination Information:

Places we discovered along the way

Places to stop and see along the way

Goals:

☐ _____
☐ _____
☐ _____
☐ _____
☐ _____
☐ _____

Would you go again?: ☐ y ☐ n   Open all year?: ☐ y ☐ n

How I felt: ☺ ☺ ☺ ☹ ☹

☐ _____
☐ _____
☐ _____
☐ _____
☐ _____

Add your favorite ticket stub, postcard, photo, stamp, decals or drawings here

www.mynaturebookadventures.com

DESTINATION:

S M T W T F S

Season Visited

Star Rating
☆☆☆☆☆

My favorite souvenir...
My favorite thing about this place is...

Why I went ...
Who I went with ...
When I went ...

What I did...
What I saw...

What I learned...

My List
- ☐
- ☐
- ☐
- ☐
- ☐
- ☐
- ☐
- ☐
- ☐
- ☐
- ☐

A laughable moment...

A surprising moment...

An unforeseeable moment...

Snapped a selfie | Location...

Took a park sign selfie? - Y | N   The weather was ...

www.mynaturebookadventures.com

Plan Your Trip:

☐ Trip Plan Completed
☐ Day Trip   ☐ Overnight Stay
Reservations required: ☐ y ☐ n
Date reservations made: _____
Confirmation #: _____
Dog friendly?: ☐ y ☐ n

Destination Information:

_____
_____

Places we discovered along the way

_____
_____
_____

Places to stop and see along the way

_____
_____

Goals:

☐ _____
☐ _____
☐ _____
☐ _____
☐ _____
☐ _____

Would you go again?: ☐ y ☐ n   Open all year?: ☐ y ☐ n

How I felt: ☺ ☺ ☺ ☹ ☹

☐ _____
☐ _____
☐ _____
☐ _____
☐ _____

Add your favorite ticket stub, postcard, photo, stamp, decals or drawings here

www.mynaturebookadventures.com

DESTINATION:

S M T W T F S

Season Visited

Star Rating
☆ ☆ ☆ ☆ ☆

My favorite souvenir...
My favorite thing about this place is...

Why I went ...
Who I went with ...
When I went ...

What I did...
What I saw...

What I learned...

A laughable moment...

A surprising moment...

An unforeseeable moment...

My List
- ☐
- ☐
- ☐
- ☐
- ☐
- ☐
- ☐
- ☐
- ☐
- ☐
- ☐

Snapped a selfie | Location...
Took a park sign selfie? - y | n   The weather was ...

www.mynaturebookadventures.com

Plan Your Trip:

☐ Trip Plan Completed
☐ Day Trip ☐ Overnight Stay
Reservations required: ☐ y ☐ n
Date reservations made: _____
Confirmation #: _____
Dog friendly?: ☐ y ☐ n

Destination Information:

_____
_____

Places we discovered along the way

_____
_____
_____

Places to stop and see along the way

_____
_____

Goals:

☐ _____
☐ _____
☐ _____
☐ _____
☐ _____
☐ _____

Would you go again?: ☐ y ☐ n   Open all year?: ☐ y ☐ n

How I felt: 😊😀😐☹️😣

☐ _____
☐ _____
☐ _____
☐ _____
☐ _____

Add your favorite ticket stub, postcard, photo, stamp, decals or drawings here

www.mynaturebookadventures.com

DESTINATION:

S M T W T F S

Season Visited

_____
Star Rating
☆☆☆☆☆

My favorite souvenir... _____
My favorite thing about this place is... _____
_____

Why I went ... _____
Who I went with ... _____
When I went ... _____
_____

What I did... _____
What I saw... _____
_____

What I learned... _____
_____
_____

A laughable moment... _____
_____
_____

A surprising moment... _____
_____
_____

An unforeseeable moment... _____
_____
_____

My List
☐ _____
☐ _____
☐ _____
☐ _____
☐ _____
☐ _____
☐ _____
☐ _____
☐ _____
☐ _____
☐ _____
☐ _____

Snapped a selfie | Location... _____
Took a park sign selfie? - y | n   The weather was ...

www.mynaturebookadventures.com

Plan Your Trip:

☐ Trip Plan Completed
☐ Day Trip   ☐ Overnight Stay
Reservations required: ☐ y ☐ n
Date reservations made: _____
Confirmation #: _____
Dog friendly?: ☐ y ☐ n

Destination Information:

_____

Places we discovered along the way

_____
_____
_____
_____

Places to stop and see along the way

_____
_____

Goals:

☐ _____
☐ _____
☐ _____
☐ _____
☐ _____
☐ _____

Would you go again?: ☐ y ☐ n   Open all year?: ☐ y ☐ n

How I felt: ☺ ☺ ☺ ☹ ☹

☐ _____
☐ _____
☐ _____
☐ _____
☐ _____

Add your favorite ticket stub, postcard, photo, stamp, decals or drawings here

www.mynaturebookadventures.com

DESTINATION:

S M T W T F S

Season Visited

Star Rating
☆☆☆☆☆

My favorite souvenir...
My favorite thing about this place is...

Why I went ...
Who I went with ...
When I went ...

What I did...
What I saw...

What I learned...

My List
- ☐
- ☐
- ☐
- ☐
- ☐
- ☐
- ☐
- ☐
- ☐
- ☐
- ☐
- ☐

A laughable moment...

A surprising moment...

An unforeseeable moment...

Snapped a selfie | Location...
Took a park sign selfie? - y | n   The weather was ...

www.mynaturebookadventures.com

Plan Your Trip:

☐ Trip Plan Completed
☐ Day Trip ☐ Overnight Stay
Reservations required: ☐ y ☐ n
Date reservations made:
Confirmation #:
Dog friendly?: ☐ y ☐ n

Places to stop and see along the way

Goals:

☐
☐
☐
☐
☐
☐

Destination Information:

Places we discovered along the way

Would you go again?: ☐ y ☐ n   Open all year?: ☐ y ☐ n

How I felt: 😊😊😐☹️☹️

☐
☐
☐
☐
☐

Add your favorite ticket stub, postcard, photo, stamp, decals or drawings here

www.mynaturebookadventures.com

DESTINATION:

S M T W T F S

Season Visited

Star Rating
☆☆☆☆☆

My favorite souvenir…
My favorite thing about this place is…

Why I went …
Who I went with …
When I went …

What I did…
What I saw…

What I learned…

A laughable moment…

A surprising moment…

An unforeseeable moment…

My List
- ☐
- ☐
- ☐
- ☐
- ☐
- ☐
- ☐
- ☐
- ☐
- ☐
- ☐
- ☐

Snapped a selfie | Location…

The weather was …

www.mynaturebookadventures.com

ADVENTURE

Like our books?
Check out some of these favorites!

- National Parks Adventure Book
- Florida State Parks Adventure Book
- Wisconsin State Parks Adventure Book
- Texas State Parks Adventure Book
- Arizona State Parks Adventure Book
- Michigan State Parks Adventure Book
- New York State Parks Adventure Book
- Indiana State Parks Adventure Book
- Our Story
- New England Lighthouses Adventure Book
- National Parks Photo Adventure Journal
- Hiking